Dear Parent:

Congratulations! Your child is taking the first steps on an exciting journey. The destination? Independent reading!

STEP INTO READING® will help your child get there. The program offers five steps to reading success. Each step includes fun stories and colorful art. There are also Step into Reading Sticker Books, Step into Reading Math Readers, Step into Reading Write-In Readers, Step into Reading Phonics Readers, and Step into Reading Phonics First Steps! Boxed Sets—a complete literacy program with something for every child.

Learning to Read, Step by Step!

Ready to Read Preschool–Kindergarten
• big type and easy words • rhyme and rhythm • picture clues
For children who know the alphabet and are eager to begin reading.

Reading with Help Preschool–Grade 1
• basic vocabulary • short sentences • simple stories
For children who recognize familiar words and sound out new words with help.

Reading on Your Own Grades 1–3
• engaging characters • easy-to-follow plots • popular topics
For children who are ready to read on their own.

Reading Paragraphs Grades 2–3
• challenging vocabulary • short paragraphs • exciting stories
For newly independent readers who read simple sentences with confidence.

Ready for Chapters Grades 2–4
• chapters • longer paragraphs • full-color art
For children who want to take the plunge into chapter books but still like colorful pictures.

STEP INTO READING® is designed to give every child a successful reading experience. The grade levels are only guides. Children can progress through the steps at their own speed, developing confidence in their reading, no matter what their grade.

Remember, a lifetime love of reading starts with a single step!

For my amazing husband, Bill
—J.G.M.

For Stina, who shares my burrow
—P.M.

With grateful acknowledgment to Lisa Bradley of the Museum of Texas Tech University for her time and expertise in reviewing this book.

Photo credit: Simpson's Glyptodont (*Glyptotherium floridanum*) carapace and tail armor courtesy of the Texas Natural Science Center, the University of Texas at Austin (p. 48)

Text copyright © 2009 by Jennifer Guess McKerley
Illustrations copyright © 2009 by Paul Mirocha

Visit us on the Web!
www.stepintoreading.com

Educators and librarians, for a variety of teaching tools, visit us at
www.randomhouse.com/teachers

Library of Congress Cataloging-in-Publication Data
McKerley, Jennifer Guess.
Amazing armadillos / by Jennifer Guess McKerley ; illustrated by Paul Mirocha. — 1st ed.
    p. cm.
ISBN 978-0-375-84352-5 (trade) — ISBN 978-0-375-94352-2 (lib. bdg.)
1. Armadillos—Juvenile literature. I. Mirocha, Paul, ill. II. Title.
QL737.E23M35 2009
599.3'12—dc22 2008035184

Printed in the United States of America

10 9 8 7 6 5 4 3 2

STEP INTO READING®

STEP 3

Amazing Armadillos

by Jennifer Guess McKerley
illustrated by Paul Mirocha

Random House 🏠 New York

The armadillo sneaks out
to hunt on a summer night.
(Say ar-muh-DIH-loh.)
Her walk is slow and clumsy.

She stands up on her back legs
to listen and sniff the air.
Uh-oh!
She smells danger.

A bobcat is on the prowl.

The armadillo knows

what to do.

Like a digging machine,

she rips the ground

with her claws.

Quickly she disappears

inside the hole.

The bobcat finally gives up.

That's good for the armadillo.

All that digging

has made her hungry.

The armadillo grunts and
hunts with her nose in the dirt.

Armadillos do not see well.
So she uses her sharp senses
of smell and hearing
to find food.

Tonight, she picks up
the scent of a beetle.
Yum!
She is so hungry
she doesn't notice
a man waiting to chase her away.

People get mad
when armadillos make holes
in their yards.
They also say armadillos stink.

The surprised armadillo squeals.
She leaps straight up—
three feet in the air.
Jumping startles her enemies
and gives her time to get away.

With a dog close behind,
she runs in a zigzag trail.
She dashes inside
a prickly bush.

Ouch!

The dog backs away

from the thorns.

But why doesn't the armadillo

feel the spikes?

She is protected by a shell

from the tip of her tail

to her nose.

"Armadillo" means
"little armored one"
in Spanish.
The armor is
made of thin bony plates
covered with tough skin.
In the center are nine narrow bands.
The skin feels like stiff leather.

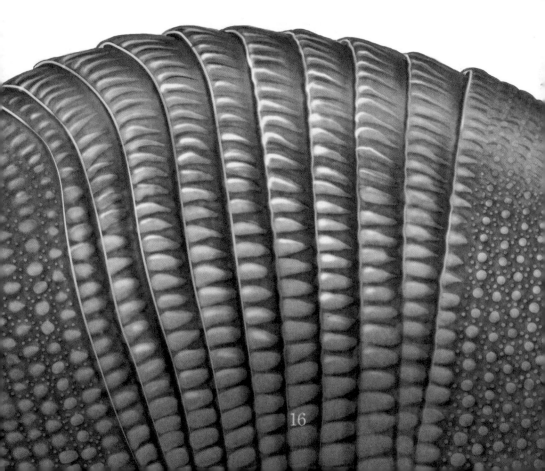

The armadillo tucks her head
into her shell.
Now her eyes are safe.
When she pulls her feet in,
her armor lowers to the ground.

Although the armor over her
shoulders and bottom is solid,
the bands in the middle move.
She curls her head to her tail.

She is a

nine-banded armadillo—

the only kind of armadillo

that lives wild

in the United States.

She is the size of a house cat.

The dog just won't give up.

Where can the armadillo go?

Ah! A fence.

She scrambles up and over.

Now the armadillo

is really hungry—and lucky.

She has landed by a garden.

She loves plowed fields,

lawns, and gardens

with soft dirt and many bugs.

Her favorite food is insects.

But she is not picky.
She will eat anything small
in her path, like fruit, lizards,
tarantulas, snails, mice,
scorpions, and bird eggs.

But what about this snake?
With a flick of her tongue,
she slurps up the snake
and swallows him whole.
The armadillo uses her dull,
round teeth only
to chew hard foods.

The armadillo smells worms
eight inches below the ground—
also fire ants.
Her claws tear the ground.
Her long tongue
darts in and out.

With each flick,
its sticky coating
and rough surface
collect hundreds of ant eggs.
Like her cousin the anteater,
she can eat 40,000 ants
in one meal.

But suddenly
she leaps backward.
Ants can't hurt her shell,
but they sting
the end of her nose
and her belly.
They even sting the skin
between her nine bands.

She will return to this hole
when insects gather again.

Now the armadillo
must cross a stream.
She breathes in
to fill her lungs.
She swallows air
to expand her belly.
Gulp.
It swells by three inches.
Then the armadillo paddles—
puffed up and floating.

Sometimes she floats on logs.

Sometimes she walks

across the bottom of the stream.

She can hold her breath

for six minutes underwater.

It's another good way to hide.

As summer turns to fall,
the armadillo digs a home.
She already has other burrows
to escape to in her hunting area.
She digs under the roots of trees
so she has a strong roof above.

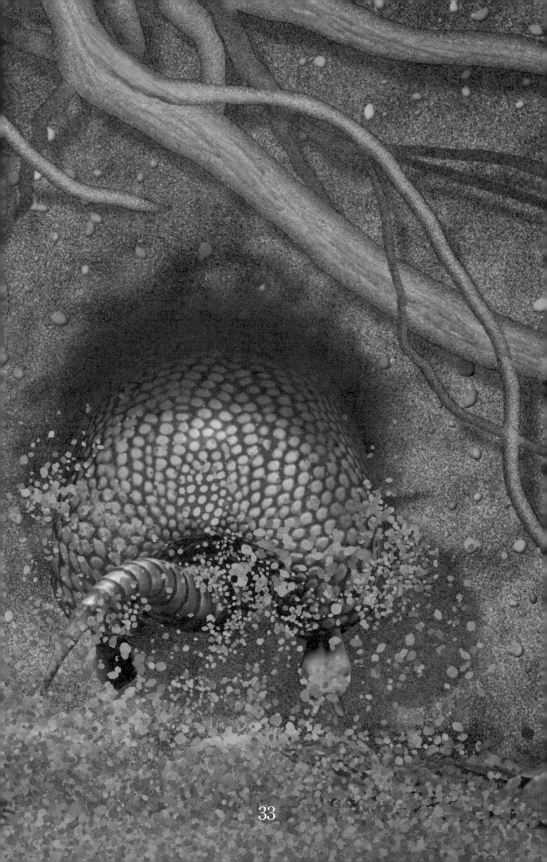

Her burrows can be
twenty feet long,
with different rooms.
They often have
several entrances.
If a skunk or another armadillo
moves in, she shares her home.

Armadillos do not like
cold weather.
That's why they mainly
live in the southern part
of the United States.
In late fall and winter,
the armadillo will hunt when
the sun is out.

Brrrr.

She runs around in circles
to warm up.

She piles leaves high

over her doors

to keep out the chill.

If it's too cold,

she sleeps a long time

in her burrow without eating.

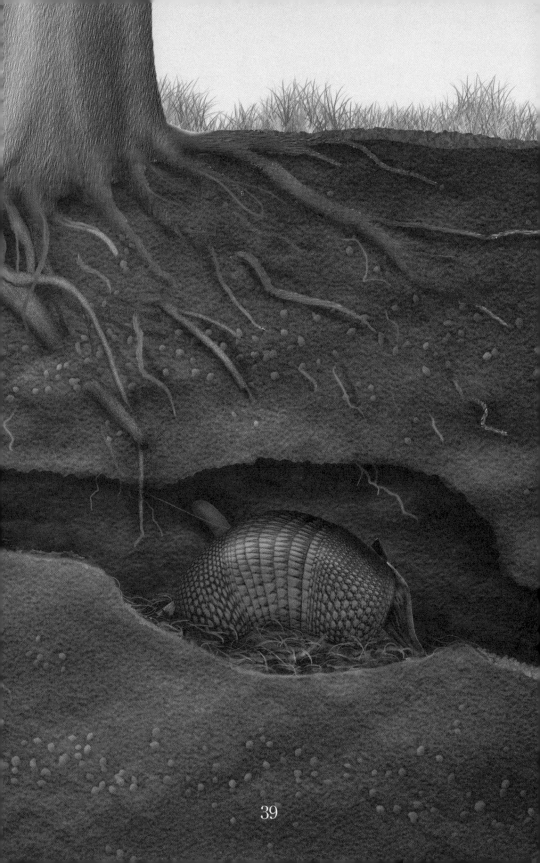

The armadillo prepares a nest
for her babies in the spring.
She carries straw and grass
with her front legs.

Then she hops backward.

She uses her tail to feel
her way into the burrow
and to the bedroom.
She made the bedroom a pit,
lower than the other rooms.

Nine-banded armadillos
always produce four babies,
or quadruplets (kwah-DROO-pluts).
The four pups are
always exactly alike.
This mom's pups are male.
They are born with
their eyes open.
They walk and play right away.

Like other mammals,
an armadillo feeds
her babies with her milk.
Yet she is the only mammal
with a shell.
Her babies' armor
feels like rubber,
but the shells will harden
as the pups grow.

In a few weeks,

she takes her pups outside.

She has lots to teach them.

Months later,

four hungry armadillos

sneak out to hunt for food.

They smell danger!

They know just what to do.

Author's Note

Twenty other kinds of armadillos live in Central and South America. They range from the pink fairy armadillo (six inches long) to the giant armadillo (five feet long, or as long as a bathtub). Fossils show that an armadillo as big as a small car once lived.

This fossil was found near the town of Ingleside, Texas, in 1939. It is thought to be about 35,000 to 50,000 years old.